Table of Contents

iWork

Pages

Pages is Apple's version of a word processor. It is part of the iWork suite of software. In many respects, it is familiar to those using other such programs. There are some key differences however. For all of the "I" software I will cover – I plan to go over the key features and how to get started. Once you know the basics – explore the program and learn

how to become a power user in no time. To the left is the first screen to greet you when you login. Notice that in the middle of the screen, you can play a Getting Started Video. I recommend watching it and then using this guide as a hard-copy reference to look back to when needed. There is also a link to watch more tutorials and how to get hands-on help at the Apple Store. Again, please use this guide a step to learn on your own and keep handy when needed. Click on the close button to get into the program. All the way to the left, on the bottom you can have the program skip this initial screen by un-checking the Show this window when Pages opens box. The next screen to appear is the **Template Chooser**. After you select the one you want to use – double-click in the document preview to open it.

There are many types of documents to choose from and there are a few choices available for each category. For **Word Processing** some of the choices include:

Blank: If you just want to start typing a document

Letters: General templates of basic letters

Envelopes: General templates of various envelops

Forms: Includes faxes and invoices

Resumes: Includes 17 different layouts of resumes

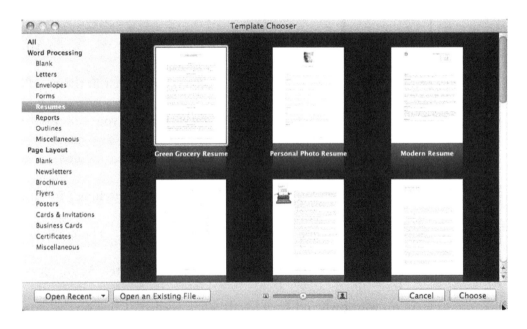

The **Resume Chooser** is shown above.

There also quite a variety of documents available under **Page Layout**. Some are unique to this program and make creating these types of documents a breeze!!! These include:

Newsletters	**Brochures**	**Flyers**
Posters	**Cards & Invitations**	**Business Cards**
Certificates		

Sample Blank Document

Above is the basic screen when you launch Pages for the first time. Every one of the icons on the screen has a specific purpose. I will go through each on the next few pages.

Toolbars buttons

Red Button – Closes the document you are working on. (Button on far left)

Yellow Button – Collapses the document down to your Dock. Document is still open and can be brought back to the main screen by clicking on the icon in the dock. (Button in the middle)

Green Button – If you resize your window, this will toggle between the smaller and the largest the document was on the screen. (Button on the far right)

View Button Options: On the right are all of the choices of items to be shown on the screen.   I have chosen Search and Show Styles Drawer. There are a few more options that can be shown. Explore!!

The next item on this top toolbar is **Full Screen**. This just hides all other items on the screen except for the page you are working on. It eliminates all other potential distractions.   To return to the normal view – press the ESC key.

 To the left is an example the **Outline Button**, which is the next item on the top toolbar.

The next item is the **Sections Button**. This adds separate sections to your document quickly.

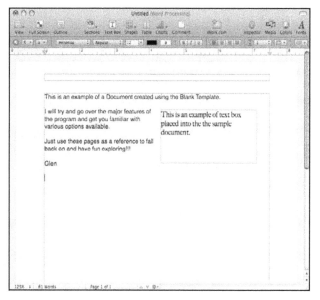

Next, is the **Text Box Button**. This allows you to create text blocks and if you want to link them to other text boxes in your document. You can move these boxes around more freely than a regular text entry.

Next to the Text Box Button is the **Shapes Button**. To the left is an example of the various shapes you can choose from. Once they are inserted, you can modify their size and location.

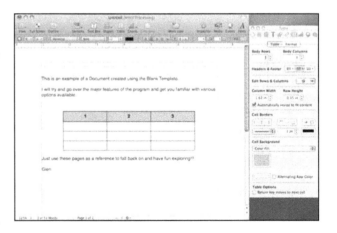

To the right is an example of a table I inserted into my document by clicking on the **Table Button**. (Table of 3 columns and 4 rows). Notice that there is a separate set of choices that pops up when you insert a table (Inspector window). You can modify the number of columns and rows, modify the cell borders and background and its header and footer. (Header is the grey area I selected to be the header in the above example.)

 Chart Button – and associated windows.

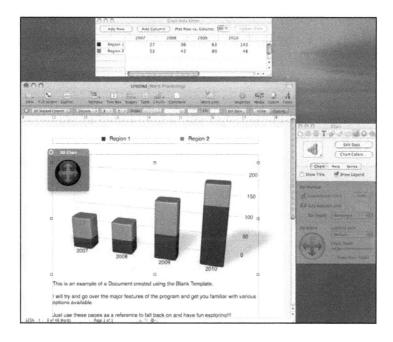

In Pages, it is easy to create 3D charts in a flash. In the center of the above example is the final product of all the data I entered and settings I chose. Notice on the top of the screen is the little spreadsheet with all the data headings and actual figures used. Notice that on the right of the document is the dialog box (Inspector Window – Chart options) to chose the type of chart and to further customize the type of chart.

 The **Comment Button** is next. This also you to add special notes to the document you are working on.

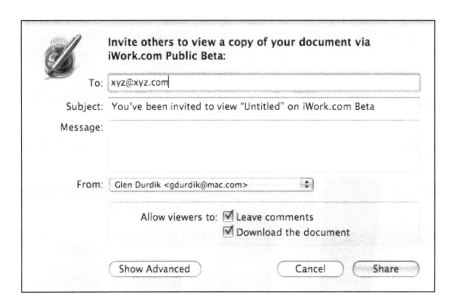 iWork.Com (BETA)

Above is a new feature that allows you to send documents to others and give them the ability to download the document or leave comments. If you click the Show Advanced Button – you can also copy it to iWork.com as a unique name and decide on download options such as Pages '09 , Pages '08, Word or PDF format.

Inspector Button (Very Useful)

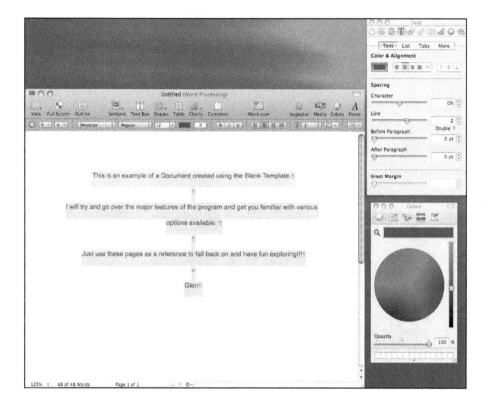

The **Inspector Button** brings up the Inspector window. This is shown on to the right of the document above. The top row of icons gives you the category of features you want to customize. These include: **Document wide settings, Layout, Object Wrapping, Text, Graphic, Metrics, Table, Chart, (Hyper) Link and QuickTime**. Text is shown above.

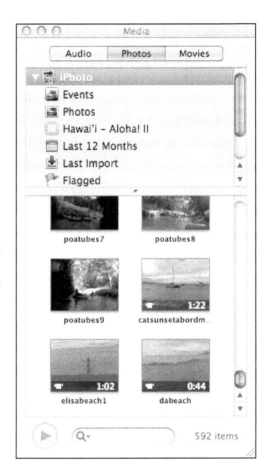

The **Media Button** shown on the right gives you access to all of your digital media from iTunes or iPhoto.

The **Color Button** simply allows you to change the color of the item you select. You are given the choice of five different palettes of color to choose from.

The **Font Button** gives you the ability to change various aspects of the type you have written in your document. The Font you use, the color and size of the font are just three choices available here.

Second Row of Buttons

Styles Drawer Button (Blue Button – Far left)

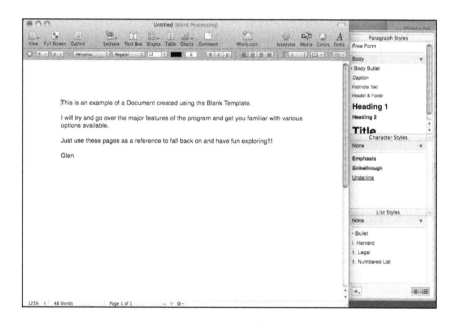

Here you can change the style of the paragraph (Body, Caption, Header or Footer, Heading, Title, etc.), the Character style (Emphasis, Strikethrough or Underline) and last the List style – (Bullet, Harvard, Legal or Numbered List).

Next to the **Styles Drawer Button** are just the **Paragraph Style Button**  and the

Character Style Button . The Paragraph options are shown on the left below and the Character options shown on the right below.

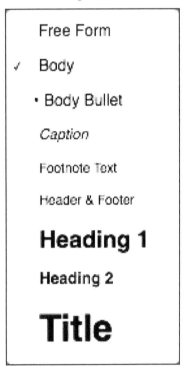

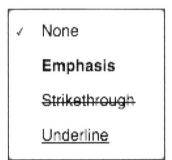

Next, are the options to modify the font's characteristics.

The first button allows you to choose the Font family. This feature is useful because it shows a preview of each font. This is shown on the right.

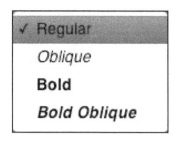

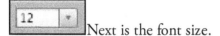 The second is used to determining the font's typeface. This is shown to the far left.

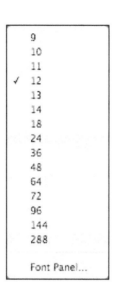

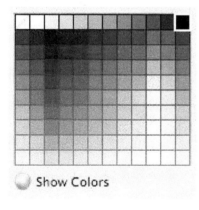 Next is the font size.

Then comes the option to change the font color.

Next to that is the option to change the color behind the text.

The letter **B** – makes the font **BOLD**. The **I** – makes the font *ITALIC*. The letter **U** makes the Font <u>UNDERLINED.</u>

This changes the text alignment. Far left – Left justified. Middle – Centered. The third button makes the alignment set to the right. The button all the way to the right makes the test justified (left and right aligned).

Next is the button to set line spacing.

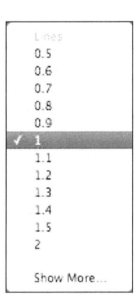

Next is the button

The last button on this row is List Style.

The last row is the Ruler. This is shown below. Notice the blue triangles on either side of the ruler. This denotes the margins of the page.

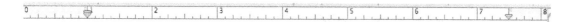

Pages – Menus

Pages Menu

About Pages	
Preferences...	⌘,
Try iWork...	
Provide Pages Feedback	
Register Pages	
Services	▶
Hide Pages	⌘H
Hide Others	⌥⌘H
Show All	
Quit Pages	⌘Q

About Pages – Tells you the version of Pages. The **Preferences...** section is discussed in detail on the following pages.

Pages Menu – Preferences - General

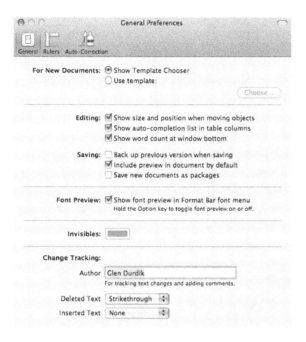

For New Documents – Allows you to use the default of opening up with the Template Chooser or your own template.

Editing – Can check off Pages to show size and position when moving objects, show auto-completion list in table columns and show word count at the window bottom.

Saving – You can choose to backup previous versions when saving, include a preview in document and last, save the new document as a package.

Font Preview – Allows you to show font a font preview in the Format Bar Font menu.

Invisibles – If turned on – this option sets the color of them. (periods, returns, tabs)

Change Tracking – Here you set the Author and how deleted text and inserted text are shown on the screen

(Strikethrough, None or Underline)

Pages – Preferences - Rulers

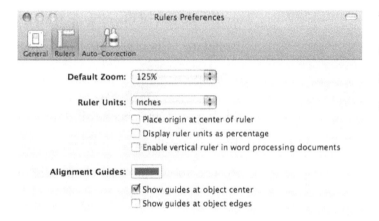

This Preference sets your choices on your default zoom, ruler units (inches for example) and alignment guides.

Pages – Preferences – Auto Correction

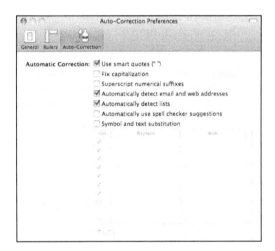

This preference tells Pages what to check for while you are typing. Note: there are seven categories and by default only three are turned on.

Pages – File Menu

```
New                          ⌘N
New from Template Chooser... ⇧⌘N

Open...                      ⌘O
Open Recent                   ▶

Close                        ⌘W
Save                         ⌘S
Save As...                   ⇧⌘S
Revert to Saved...

Reduce File Size

Save as Template...

Page Setup...                ⇧⌘P
Print...                     ⌘P
```

New and **New from Template Chooser...** allows you to create a new document. **Open** allows you to open a document from a location that you select. **Open Recent** – Pages remembers the last documents you have been working on. This is a quick and easy way to access the last saved version of your document. **Close** closes the document. **Note:** The program will warn you if you DID NOT save the most recent changes. **Save** saves the work with the name it is already saved as. **Save As...** Gives you the option to save your doc with a different name or a different location. **Revert to Saved...** rolls back your document to the last previous SAVED state.

Reduce File Size – If you imported large graphics... this option reduces their size within the document. You must save your document once to use this feature. **Save as Template** – Allows you to create your own template for future use. **Page Setup** and **Print** determine printer settings and once configured – to print the document to a printer.

Pages – Edit Menu

Undo Typing	⌘Z
Redo	⇧⌘Z
Cut	⌘X
Copy	⌘C
Paste	⌘V
Paste and Match Style	⌥⇧⌘V
Delete	
Delete Page...	
Clear All	
Duplicate	⌘D
Select All	⌘A
Deselect All	⇧⌘A
Track Changes	
Mail Merge...	
Find	▶
Spelling	▶
Proofreading	▶
Writing Tools	▶
Special Characters...	

Undo and **Redo** – Undo allows you to take one step back in your typing. (insert a word or sentence and then you decide you want to delete it.) **Cut** – Deletes the selection you have highlighted. **Copy** – Copies the selection you want to use elsewhere. **Paste** and **Paste and Match Style** – inserts what you have copied. Paste and Match Style pastes all formatting. **Delete** and **Delete Pages** – remove what you select. **Clear All** is used when you have inserted a Chart and what to delete a selection of data. **Select all** – highlights all of the text you chose. Good if you want to change the font on one paragraph for example. **Deselect All** – removes Select All if you just chose that. **Track Changes** – Used to track the changes of your document. **Mail Merge** is used to combine a document of names and addresses with a letter that needs to be addressed to many different people.

Pages – Edit Menu – Find Submenu

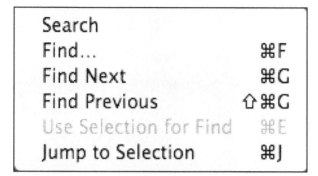

The **Find** Command allows you to search for a word either by using Search or Find…. The **Find…** command is combined with the ability to REPLACE any word in your document. You might want to change dog to canine everywhere in your document for example.

Pages – Edit Menu – Spelling Submenu

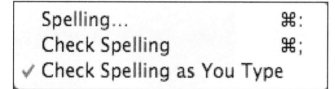

This is used to check you document for common spelling errors.

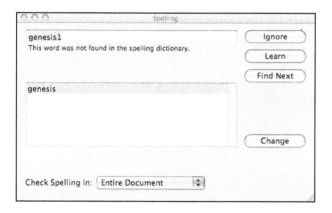

To the right is an example of the Spelling command. Genesis1 is recognized as a typo and suggests Genesis as a correct spelling. Click on Change to correct it. Ignore it does not make a change. Learn adds the word to the application's dictionary.

Pages – Edit Menu – Proofreading Submenu

Proofreader...
Proofread
Proofread as You Type

This is a tool that gives general suggestions to improve your document's wording. You do not have to accept the program's choice.

This is an example of the **Proofreading** function in action. Notice it states that the first word of a sentence should be capitalized.

○ ○ ○   Proofreading

Alternatives

Genesis1   (Next)

genesis1   (Correct)

Capitalization error. The first word of a sentence should be capitalized.
Consider 'Genesis1' instead of 'genesis1'.

Pages – Edit Menu – Writing Tools Submenu

```
┌─────────────────────────────────────────────────┐
│  Look Up in Dictionary and Thesaurus            │
│                                                  │
│  Search in Spotlight                             │
│  Search in Google                                │
│  Search in Wikipedia                             │
│                                                  │
│  Show Statistics                                 │
└─────────────────────────────────────────────────┘
```

This is a VERY useful feature. **Look Up in Dictionary and Thesaurus** are found on your hard drive. **Spotlight** searches your entire hard drive for the inclusion of the word you are searching for. **Search in Google** and **Wikipedia** goes out and searches the web for more information on the word you are looking up. **Show Statistics** gives you info on what is contained in your document (Info tab) and various settings and dimensions of your document (Document Tab)

Pages – Insert Menu

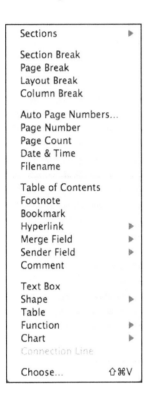

This menu is broken down into five sections. The first deals with inserting a "break" between a section, page, layout or column. The next section deals with page numbers, date and time or inserting a filename. The third section deals with a variety of topics that include: table of contents, footnotes, bookmarks, hyperlinks, merge field or sender field and last, a comment. The next to last section deals with inserting a text box, shape, table, function, chart or connection line. The last option – Choose... allows you to manually insert what you want. A picture for example.

Pages – Format Menu

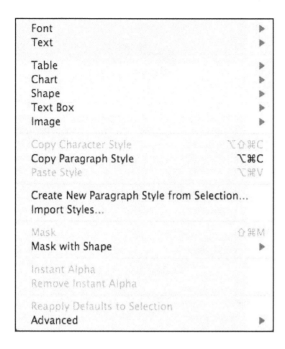

This Menu allows you to change the characteristics on many of the items in your work. These include font or text changes, table, chart, shape, text box and image changes as well. In the section below this group, you can copy a character or paragraph style and paste (apply) it to another section. You can also import a style here as well. **Mask** and **Mask with shape** allows you to apply a crop or a distinct shape over your graphic. **Instant Alpha** – makes the color of your choice to be transparent.

Pages – Format Menu – Advanced Submenu

Capture Pages...
Manage Pages...

Define Default Graphic Style

Make Default Chart Type

Define as Placeholder Text   ^⌥⌘T
Enable Placeholder Text Authoring

Define as Media Placeholder   ^⌥⌘I

Make Master Objects Selectable
Move Object to Section Master

Capture... and **Manage Pages...** allows you to single out one or a few pages of your current document for future use. You can also set the default for the graphic style, chart type, placeholder text or Media here as well. Master Objects are items such as logos that you might want to use throughout your work. Here you can make these selectable.

Pages – Arrange Menu

An item can be either "in front of" or "behind" another graphic for example. The first section allows you to bring this item forward one, back one, to the bottom or to the top of the "layers." You can also send an object to the background here.

Pages – View Menu

Page Thumbnails	⌥⌘P
Search	⌥⌘F
Show Styles Drawer	⇧⌘T
Hide Rulers	⌘R
Hide Format Bar	⇧⌘R
Show Comments	
Show Layout	⇧⌘L
Show Invisibles	⇧⌘I
Show Document Outline	
Zoom	▶
Hide Inspector	⌥⌘I
New Inspector	
Show Colors	⇧⌘C
Show Adjust Image	
Show Media Browser	
Show Document Warnings	
Enter Full Screen	⌥⌘U
Hide Toolbar	⌥⌘T
Customize Toolbar...	

This menu allows you to set various elements in your work - it is either hidden or shown on the screen. You can also enter Full Screen mode here and customize your toolbar as well.

Pages – Window Menu

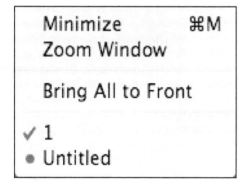

Minimize – takes your document and places it in your dock. It is no longer on the screen. To bring it back up, click on the icon for it in your dock. **Note:** Documents are placed to the right of the white bar in your dock. Note: In the example to the left – there are two documents. 1 and Untitled. You can go through all open documents by highlighting the one you want in this menu.

Pages – Share Menu

This menu allows you to share your work in variety of ways. **iWork.com, email or iWeb are three ways of making it accessible via the Internet.**

Pages – Share Menu – Export Submenu

If you want to change the file type – this is one way of doing so. Notice that you can save the document as a PDF (portable document format), Word, RTF or plain text. In the example to the left – notice that you can control the quality of the PDF and give it a password. If you click in Next… it gives you the normal Save dialog box.

Pages – Help Menu

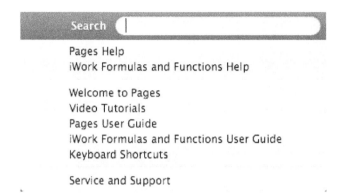

Got a question? Want to more deeply explore the features of Pages? This is where to go.

That's it for Pages. Pretty cool huh? As I mentioned, this is not meant to be a super-guide to Pages. I just want you to see what it is and where everything is located. EXPLORE and have some fun learning this word processor/page layout editor from Apple.

iWork:

Numbers

Numbers is neat application designed to make using spreadsheets a whole lot easier. As with Pages, I will go into detail of the toolbar choices and what is available in each menu. The first screen you will see when you launch Numbers is the Welcome window. (You can have this not come up by un-checking the box next to "Show this window when Numbers opens.") As with Pages, this window gives you the opportunity to see various aspects of Numbers and tutorials on certain topics. This manual is here to get you started and used a reference when not near a computer or just prefer reading a hard copy over a short video clip.

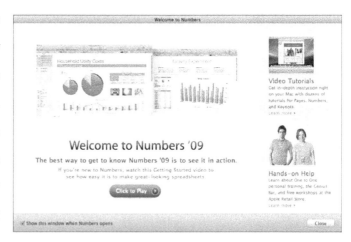

The **Template Chooser** is the next screen that will appear if you click on the close button on the far right of the window. Just like Pages, there are many to choose from. These

templates make creating important work or personal spreadsheets easy to create. Above is an example of the Personal Finance choices. If you find one you want to use – double click on it. Here are the choices available to you....

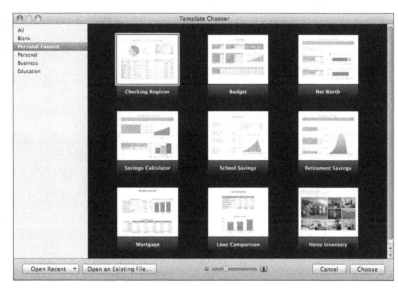

Blank: Start for "square one" and start using it without any template help.

Personal Finance: Checking Register, Budget, Net Worth, Savings Calculator, School savings, Retirement Savings, Mortgage, Loan Comparison, Home Inventory.

Personal: Workout Tracker, Weight Tracker, Baby Record, Event Planner, Dinner Party, Garden Journal, Home Improvement, Comparisons, Travel Planner, Team Organization.

Business: Employee Schedule, Invoice, Expense Report, Financials, Return on Investment.

Education: Science Lab, Gravity Lab, Math quiz, Grade Book.

I am sure that there is one template mentioned above that will make your life easier. You can also chose **Open a Recent document** or **Open an Existing File by clicking on their**

button on the bottom of this window. You can also zoom in on a template by moving the slider found in the middle of the window on the very bottom. Click **Choose** to select the one you want to cancel to start without any template.

Sample Blank Document

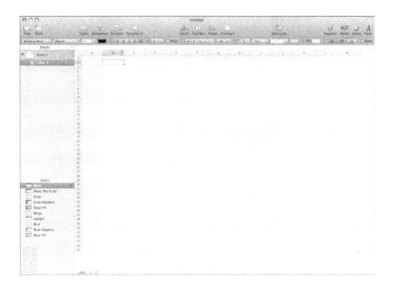

Red Button – Closes the document you are working on. (Button on far left)

Yellow Button – Collapses the document down to your Dock. Doc is still open and can be brought back to the main screen by clicking on the icon on the dock. (Button in the middle)

Green Button – If you resize your window, this will toggle between the smaller and the largest the document was on the screen. (Button on the far right)

The **View** button on toolbar below the three colored buttons allows you to decide what elements you want to be shown on the screen. The six choices available to you are shown on the right.

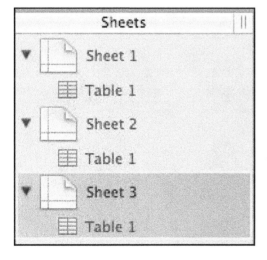

The **Sheet** button adds a new "sheet" or "workspace" every time you click on it. To the left is an example of a document with 3 Sheets.

The **Table** button determines what type of table you are using. Numbers places the new table at the bottom of your screen.

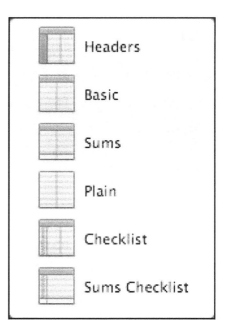

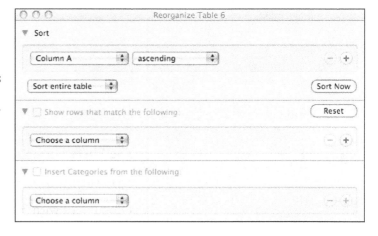

The **Reorganize** button allows you to sort you data in a table. This is shown to the right.

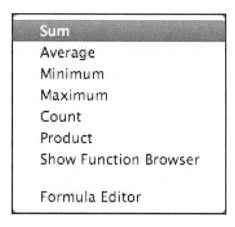

The **Function** button allows you to insert easily commonly used formulas used in a spreadsheet. Show Function Browser brings up a very comprehensive list of available formulas to choose from. Formula Editor allows you to insert and create your own formulas.

| Sum |
| Average |
| Minimum |
| Maximum |
| Count |
| Product |
| Show Function Browser |
| Formula Editor |

The **Formula List** button shows all formulas used in your document and their result. This is shown to below.

Formula List	Find & Replace...	
Location	Results	Formula
▼ Sheet 1		
▼ Table 1		
A9	205	=SUM(A2:A8)
▼ Table 6		
C11	0	=SUMIF(A,TRUE,C)

The **Chart** button allows you to set what type of chart you want to create from the data you select. The types of charts available to you are shown below.

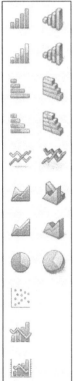

The **Text Box** button allows you to create a box that can "float" anywhere on your screen.

The **Shapes** button allows you to insert various types of shapes into your document. The shapes available are shown to the right.

The **Comment** button allows you to insert notes about the work you are doing in the spreadsheet.

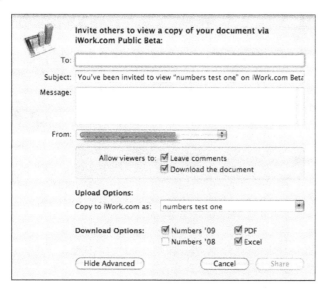 **iWork.com** (Beta) is a tool to share your documents with other people. The options available to you are shown below. **Note** that you can allow the user to download the document or save it as document type other then Numbers '09. (This option is available if you show Advanced)

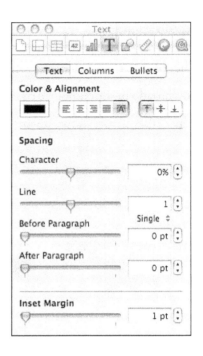

The **Inspector button** brings up a wide variety of options to modify the data in your file. In the example to the right, the Text Inspector is chosen.

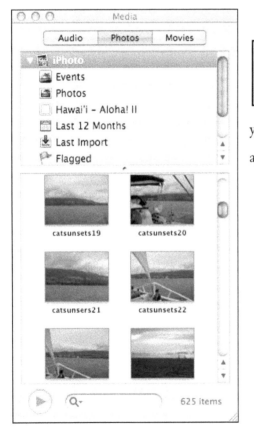

The **Media button** shown to the left – gives you access to all of your media stored in your iLife applications (iTunes and iPhoto for example)

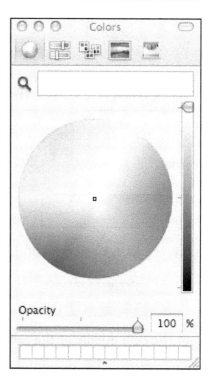

The **Color button** gives you the option to change the color on the item you have highlighted. Notice there are five different color schemes to choose from (top of the Colors window).

The last button on this first row of buttons is the **Fonts button**. Here you are given many choices of ways to modify the font on your screen. This window is shown below.

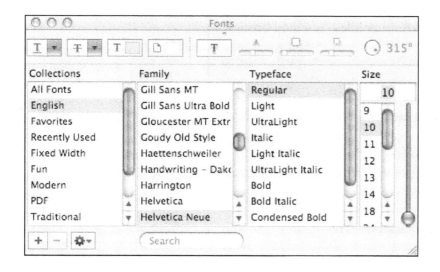

Second row of buttons.

Here you are given four characteristics to choose from to modify your text. **Font family, typeface, font size and color.**

These buttons determine the **alignment of your text** on the screen. Left, Center, Right, Justified and Auto Align are your five choices.

These buttons also set alignment. However, your **choices are top of the cell, middle of the cell, bottom of your cell or wrap the text**. Wrap the text allows you to have a long formula or sentence and the program will automatically go to the next line of text once it reaches the end of the cell. (If the cell were too small for the word Automobile – it would break it into two lines.)

These buttons format the number you highlight as one of the following - (from left to right) number with two decimal points, currency, percentage, a checkbox (turns cell into a box with a check it) and last a wide variety of choices via Custom. This is shown to the right.

These buttons set the number of decimal places.

 These buttons set the characteristics of the cell borders.

This button sets the cell's fill. It does not have to be just white all the time.

From left to right - sets the number of header columns and when they display, sets the number of header rows and when they display, sets the number of footer rows and how they are displayed. **Name** determines if you want the select and display the table name.

Numbers – Menus

Numbers – Numbers Menu

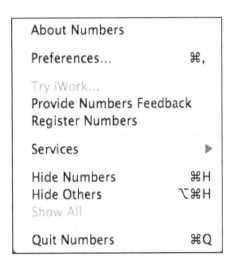

The Numbers Menu's first item – **About Numbers** tells you the version of the software you are running. The next item - Preferences is discussed below.

Numbers – Numbers Menu – Preferences - General

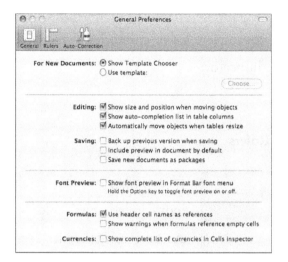

For New Documents – Sets whether you have the default Template Chooser or use you own template whenever you start Numbers.

Editing – there are three items – decide if you want to show the size and position when moving objects, show auto-completion list in table columns and if you want to have the program automatically move objects when tables resize.

Saving – Here you chose to have the program back up the previous version when saving, include preview in document by default and last… save new documents a packages.

Font Preview – Allows you to have font preview in the Format Bar font menu shown or not.

Formulas - Here you decide if you want header cell names as references and to show a warning if formulas reference empty cells.

Currencies – Just determines if you want a complete list of currencies in the Cells Inspector.

Numbers – Numbers Menu – Preferences - Rulers

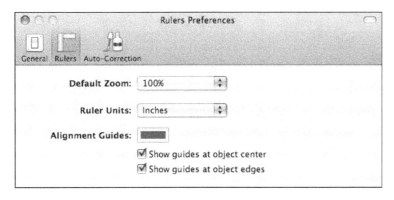

This window sets the default zoom, ruler units, color of the alignment guides and whether or not you want to show guides at the object center and or edges.

Numbers – Numbers Menu – Preferences – Auto Correction

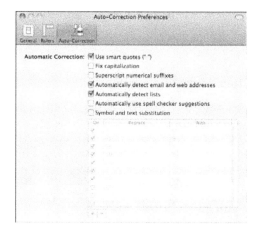

This window sets what automatic corrections you want Numbers to change. **Note** that by default all options are NOT checked off.

Numbers – File Menu

New	⌘N
New from Template Chooser...	⇧⌘N
Open...	⌘O
Open Recent	▶
Close	⌘W
Save	⌘S
Save As...	⇧⌘S
Revert to Saved...	
Reduce File Size	
Save as Template...	
Show Print View	
Print...	⌘P

New or **New from Template Chooser** – Creates a new document to work on.

Open – Opens a saved document.

Open Recent – Numbers stores a short list of documents that were recently worked on. This is an easy why to start where you left off on a document you are currently working on.

Close – Closes the document you are working on. If you did not save your last changes – you will be prompted to save your work.

Save – Saves your changes over your previous work in the document.

Save As... allows you to save a new file and keep the old one. You can also save the document elsewhere here.

Revert to Saved - Reverts your document to the last saved version.

Reduce File Size - If you inserted a lot of graphics – this option will save them at smaller sizes in your document.

Save as Template… - If you want to use the formulas and other work created in a document for future use – this saves it as a template in the My Templates folder.

Show Print View - Shows you on the screen how your work will be printed. (Spreadsheet goes onto two pages for example might not be noticed if this is off)

Print – Prints the current document. You are given the option to print the current sheet, all sheets and if you want to include a list of all formulas in the document.

Numbers – Edit Menu

Undo Hide Table Name	⌘Z
Redo	⇧⌘Z
Cut	⌘X
Copy	⌘C
Paste	⌘V
Paste and Match Style	⌥⇧⌘V
Paste Values	
Delete	
Delete Row	
Delete Column	
Clear All	
Mark for Move	⇧⌘X
Move	⇧⌘V
Duplicate	⌘D
Select All	⌘A
Deselect All	⇧⌘A
Find	▶
Spelling	▶
Special Characters...	

Undo – Removes the list item you added top your document.

Redo – Adds back the last Undo.

Cut – Deletes item from your work.

Copy – Copies the items your have selected and holds it in memory until you copy another item.

Paste – Pastes or adds what you just copied into your work where you placed your cursor.

Paste and Match Styles – Copies over all formatting associated with the data you copied.

Paste Values – Pastes just the results of your formulas.

Delete/Delete Row/Delete Column – Removes what you have selected from your document.

Clear All - Removes all data in the cell/row/column you have selected.

Mark for Move – Highlight what you want moved to another location in the document. A red outline then appears around the area.

Move – Select the cell you want to move the "Mark for Move" and select this option to move the items.

Duplicate – Allows you to copy items other then text – a chart for example.

Select All/Deselect all – Highlights all items on the screen or "un" Highlights in your document.

Find – Allows you to search your document for a specific item. You are also given the ability to "Find and Replace" the item as well.

Spelling – Gives you the option to check spelling manually, the whole document or spell check while you type.

Numbers – Table Menu

Add Row Above	⌥↑
Add Row Below	⌥↓
Add Column Before	⌥←
Add Column After	⌥→
Delete Row	
Delete Column	
Header Rows	▶
Header Columns	▶
Freeze Header Rows	
Freeze Header Columns	
Footer Rows	▶
Resize Rows to Fit Content	
Resize Columns to Fit Content	
Unhide All Rows	
Unhide All Columns	
Enable All Categories	
Merge Cells	
Split into Rows	
Split into Columns	
Distribute Rows Evenly	
Distribute Columns Evenly	
Allow Border Selection	
Show Reorganize Panel	

Need to modify the characteristics of your table? Here is a where to look. Adding or deleting columns or rows, determining the number of header rows and columns, freezing header rows and columns, resizing rows and columns to fit content, hide or unhide rows and columns, merge cells, splitting data into rows or columns, distributing rows or columns evenly or allowing border selection. The last option brings up the Reorganize Panel.

Numbers – Insert Menu

This Menu allows you to insert any one of the following: Sheet, Table, Chart, Shape, Text Box, Function, Fill, Date and Time, Filename, Page Number, Page Count, Comment, Column Break or a Hyperlink. Other allows you to insert or items such as a picture not in iPhoto.

Numbers – Format Menu

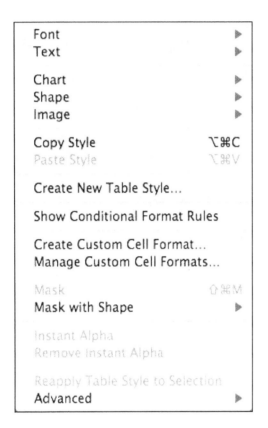

This menu allows you to change the characteristics of several different elements in your document. Font, text, chart (type, X-axis, Y-axis, hide or unhide legend), shape, or image. You can copy and paste a style, create a new table style, show conditional format rules, create custom cell formats and manage them, mask or mask with a shape. Instant Alpha allows you to take parts of a picture transparent in order to remove its background. Advanced gives you the ability to capture tables and then manage them.

Numbers – Arrange Menu

This menu gives you the ability to set how your items appear on the screen. Think of you document as having many layers. You can place a picture behind another object or align or distribute the objects. You can also flip the item horizontally or vertically, lock them or group or then ungroup a few different elements into single unit.

Numbers – View Menu

Show Print View	⌥⌘P
Show Layout	⇧⌘L
Show Rulers	⌘R
Hide Comments	
Hide Format Bar	⇧⌘R
Zoom	▶
Show Inspector	⌥⌘I
New Inspector	
Hide Colors	⇧⌘C
Show Adjust Image	
Hide Media Browser	
Show Document Warnings	
Show Function Browser	
Hide Formula List	⌥⌘F
Hide Toolbar	⌥⌘T
Customize Toolbar...	

This menu simply allows you to decide what you want to see on the screen. Print view, rulers, comments, inspector, and colors, adjust image, media browser, document warnings, function browser, formula list or hide or customize a toolbar.

Numbers – Window Menu

Minimize   ⌘M
Zoom Window

Bring All to Front

✓ numbers test one

Minimize – Places your current window into the dock. Click on the icon in the dock to bring it back.

Zoom window – Makes you document take up the entire screen.

Bring All to Front – If you have more than one application open – you might have many different files open at once. If you select this option – all of you Numbers documents will be brought to the front of the other documents.

If you have more then one document open, you would see more than the one checked off in my example.

Numbers – Share Menu

In this menu, you can share you work in a few interesting ways. iWork.com was mentioned earlier; send it via email or to iWeb for a webpage. You can also export it to a variety of formats including – PDF, Excel or CSV.

Numbers – Help Menu

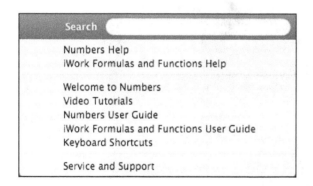

Need online help on items not discussed in detail in this manual? You are in the right place. Here you will find video tutorials, a user guide, formulas and functions user guide and keyboard shortcuts

Now you are ready to manage your finances or become the next CFO at a Fortune 500 company. Numbers is a great new way to look at spreadsheets – I hope you agree.

iWork

Keynote

Keynote is not your ordinary presentation software. Those of you that have used other programs – will find many of the features the same. But – there are many interesting and useful additions that make this software easier and more fun to use. As with the other applications, I will first discuss the toolbars and then menus found in Keynote. Let me start by showing you what happens when you first launch the application.

Note that it is slightly different then the first two applications I discussed. The Template Chooser is replaced with the **Theme Chooser...** for one. There are **44 different themes** to choose from. **PLEASE note** – If you move your mouse over a chosen template – further examples of slides in that theme are shown. Each them shows seven different slide examples.

You can also access recent files here or open an older file via this screen. To choose one, double-click on the icon or click on the Choose button on the bottom right of the screen. Slide size can be set at 800 x 600 or 1024 x 768.

Above is an example of the first screen in your presentation. If you see an element that states, "Double-click to edit" – perform that action to modify it. Now lets get into the toolbars…

 The **New button** adds a slide to your document.

 The **Play button** plays the entire presentation or part of it if want.

 The **View button** allows you to set what aids is shown on the screen. The choices are shown below.

The **Guides button** brings up the screen shown to the left.

Don't like the theme of your presentation? Clicking on this button brings up a small preview of all available themes. If you click you mouse over one – the template change will take place. The list of available themes is shown on the next page.

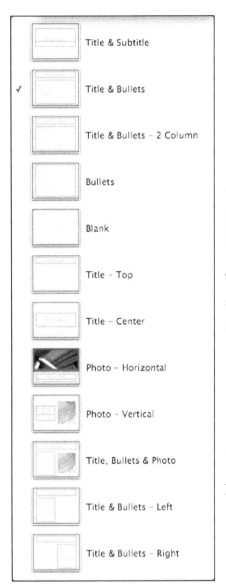

Most slides are created with certain elements in them. The **Masters button** gives you access to 12 different types. These choices are shown to the left.

This button adds a free-floating text box in your document.

The **Shapes button** gives you the ability add one of 15 different shapes. The item at the bottom of the list allows you to create a custom shape. The different options are shown to the right.

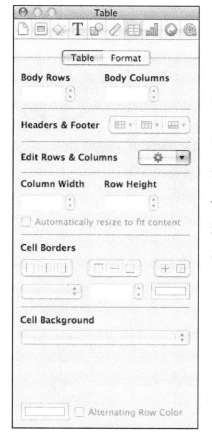

The **Table button** gives you the ability to insert a table into your presentation. When you choose this option – you are given access to the Table Inspector. This window is what you use to modify the characteristics of the table (not the data).

The **Charts button** allows you to insert a chart into your presentation. The available options are shown to the right.

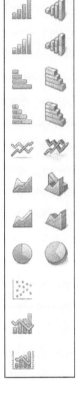

 The **Comment button** allows you to add a free-floating yellow note.

This button allows you to share or give someone the ability to download the document you choose. If you click on Show Advanced – you decide what file formats you want it to be (Keynote '09, PDF or PowerPoint for example)

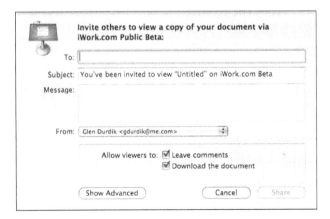

The **Mask button** deals with images in your document. Notice the slide below. The complete picture takes up the entire slide. However, because of the mask only the part I want to be seen will be on screen. Notice there is an Edit Mask slider when using this feature.

 The **Alpha button** allows you to remove a color of your choice in your picture to make it transparent.

These buttons deal with elements in you document. Think of your document as set of layers with pieces of text or pictures in them. **Group and Ungroup** – allows you to take a few objects and make them "one" in your document. Now you can move this whole group at once. There maybe a picture you want behind some text or other picture. Click on the object and click **Front to bring it forward or Back to set it below the other item.**

The **Inspector button** brings up the window shown to right. Here you nine different categories of characteristics to modify. We saw the Table window earlier. In the example, the Document tab is selected.

The **Media button** gives you access to all of your iTunes music, iPhoto pictures or movies found on you Mac.

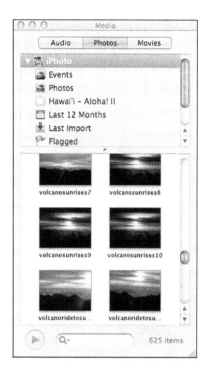

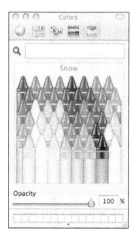

The **Colors button** allows you to change the color of the item you clicked on. Notice that there are five different sets of color schemes. In the example to the right – I chose the option all the way to the right.

The **Fonts button** gives you access wide variety of ways to modify your text. This window is shown on the next page.

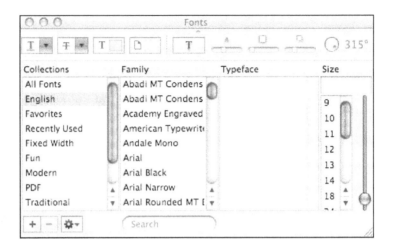

Second Row

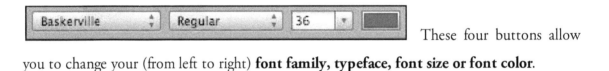 These four buttons allow you to change your (from left to right) **font family, typeface, font size or font color.**

 B makes the text **BOLD**. I makes the text *ITALIC*. U makes the text UNDERLINED.

These buttons determine **text alignment**. The choices are left, middle, right or justified.

This button determines **line spacing**.

This button allows you to **insert columns** into your text.

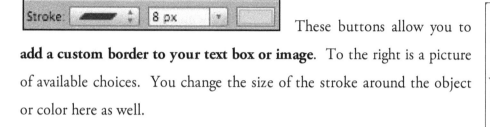 This button is very useful. If your text is too long for a text box – **this option will reduce your text so that it does fit neatly into the text box.**

 These buttons allow you to **add a custom border to your text box or image.** To the right is a picture of available choices. You change the size of the stroke around the object or color here as well.

These buttons deal with what is inside an object (Fill and Opacity) and give you the option of adding a shadow or reflection. A circle with a shadow and reflection is shown below.

Keynote – Menus

Keynote – Keynote Menu

About Keynote	
Preferences...	⌘,
Try iWork...	
Provide Keynote Feedback	
Register Keynote	
Services	▶
Hide Keynote	⌘H
Hide Others	⌥⌘H
Show All	
Quit Keynote	⌘Q

This Menu has two important items. The first – is **About Keynote**. This tells you want version of the software you are running. The second is **Preferences**.... There are six different categories of items to modify here. They are discussed separately below.

Keynote – Keynote

Menu – Preferences - General

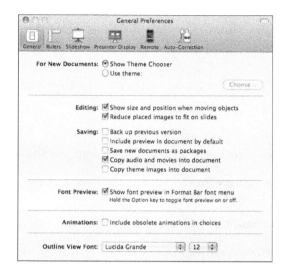

For New Documents – Allows you to chose between having the default Theme Chooser or your own theme come up whenever you create a new document.

Editing – Here you can decide if you want to show the size and position when moving objects and whether or not you want the program to reduce placed images to fit onto the slide.

Saving – Back up previous version – saves an old copy of your work when you save a new version.   Include preview in document by default – includes a small PDF version of your file for previewing purposes.

Save new documents as packages – if used – you can have access to the raw source files or XML files

Copy audio and movies into document – Saves all media files associated with the document – in the document. This is useful because you might forget to bring the media files with Keynote document for a presentation. This way if it is checked off (by default) all files are in one place.

Copy theme images into document – needed if you are going to use your document on a Mac that does not have your chosen template on it.

Font Preview – Decide if you want to show font preview in the Format Bar font menu

Animations – Decide if you want obsolete animations in choices

Outline View Font – Chose what font you want for the Outline view.

Keynote – Keynote

Menu – Preferences - Rulers

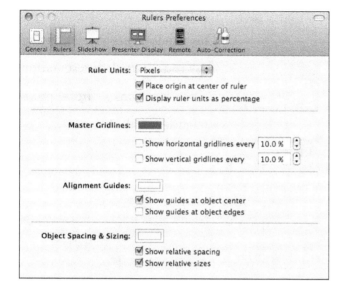

Ruler Units – Can be in pixels, centimeters or inches. You the choice of placing the origin at the center of ruler and whether or not or not to display ruler units as a percentage.

Master Gridlines – Sets its color and were you want it placed (10.0% by default).

Alignment Guides –Sets its color and if you want to show the guides at object center (on by default) and/or edges.

Object Spacing and Sizing – Sets is color and if you want to show relative spacing and or relative sizes.

Keynote – Keynote

Menu – Preferences - Slideshow

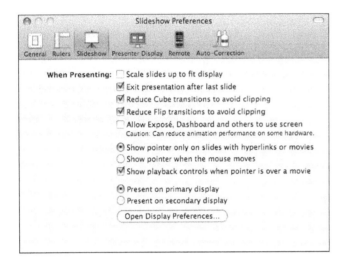

This window sets a lot of settings for you actual presentation. These options are pretty straightforward.

Keynote – Keynote

Menu – Preferences – Presentation Display

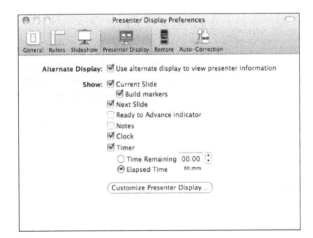

This window allows you to setup a second display for the presenter (if you have one) and what is to be only seen by this person.

Keynote – Keynote

Menu – Preferences – Remote

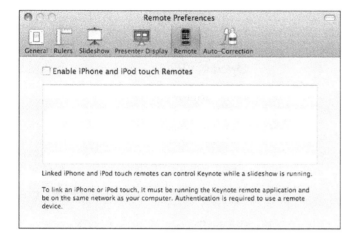

If you have an iPhone or iPod Touch – you can have it set to be a remote control for Keynote.

Keynote – Keynote

Menu – Preferences – Auto Correction

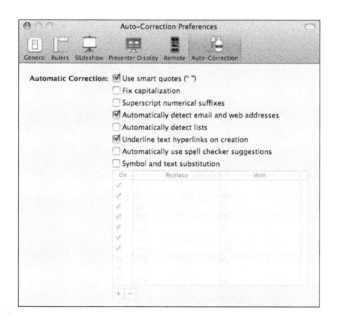

This window sets what the program will automatically correct if typed incorrectly. Notice that there are only three turned on by default.

Keynote – File Menu

```
New                          ⌘N
New from Theme Chooser...
Open...                      ⌘O
Open Recent               ▶

Close                        ⌘W
Save                         ⌘S
Save As...                 ⇧⌘S
Revert to Saved...
Export...

Reduce File Size

Record Slideshow
Clear Recording...

Choose Theme...
Save Theme...

Print...                     ⌘P
```

New / New from Theme Chooser... creates a new document.

Open – Opens a dialog box to find a saved document.

Open Recent – This program remembers a small number of recently accessed files. This is the fastest way to access current projects you are working on.

Close – Closes the document. Note – If you did not save any changes – you will be asked to save them.

Save – Writes over the last saved version.

Save As... Gives you the ability to save your work elsewhere or keep the old version you originally opened by saving a new presentation under a different name.

Revert to Saved... Takes you back to the point at which you opened the document you are working on. Back to saved "Square One."

Export – You can export your presentation as a QuickTime movie, PPT file, PDF file, a set of images, HTML files or for an iPod.

Reduce File Size – If you placed large media files into your work – this option sets out to reduce the file size of the media.

Record Slideshow – Allows you to record via microphone to your presentation.

Clear Recording... Clears your audio recording.

Choose Theme... Allows you to change the theme you currently are using.

Save Theme... Allows you to save a custom theme you created for future use.

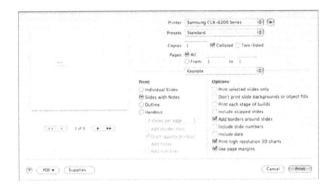

Print... Prints the current presentation – just the way you want it. I included a sample print menu from Keynote to show what is available. (Sample on the left)

Keynote – Edit Menu

Undo Move	⌘Z
Redo	⇧⌘Z
Cut	⌘X
Copy	⌘C
Paste	⌘V
Paste and Match Style	⌥⇧⌘V
Delete	
Clear All	
Duplicate	⌘D
Select All	⌘A
Deselect All	⇧⌘A
Find	▶
Spelling	▶
Special Characters...	

Undo – Reverts your work to just before your last addition. There are multiple Undos.

Redo – Puts back what you just Undoed.

Cut – Deletes the highlighted text or object.

Copy – Copies the highlighted text or object.

Paste – Takes what you just copied and pasted it into your work at the location of your cursor.

Paste and Match Style – Pastes test exactly as it was formatted when you copied it.

Delete – Removes the item you select.

Clear All – basically same as above.

Duplicate – Copies then pastes a graphic (not text) into your work.

Select All – Highlights **ALL** elements on your current slide. Useful if you want to move everything or perhaps delete everything.

Find – Allows you to search your document for a certain word. It actually brings up Find and Replace – you can find a word and potentially replace it document wide. You are given a Simple option or an Advanced Option (adds search notes and Match Case and Whole word only searches)

Spelling – Spell checks your document. You can also turn OFF the feature of automatically spell-checking your document here.

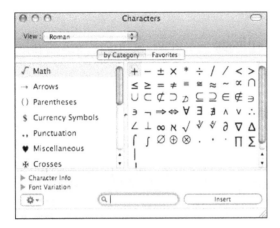

Special Characters – Here you can find unique or useful symbols that can be added to your work. Find what you like and just click on Insert.

Keynote – Insert Menu

This menu allows you to insert a wide variety of items into your presentation. The one that is most unfamiliar to users is **Smart Build. This involves adding transitions to the images you insert into the document.** If you insert two pictures here for example and you chose Dissolve – the first picture will slowly disappear on you screen and then bring up the second.

Keynote – Slide Menu

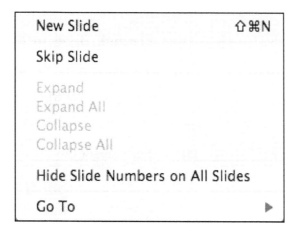

This menu deals with slides as a whole. You can add a slide, decide to "skip" a slide in your presentation (not shown on the screen when you present) or add slide numbers to all of your slides.

Keynote – Format Menu

This menu deals with changing characteristics of the element you are working on. This could be table, text or perhaps a chart. You can also copy styles and animations through this menu. You can mask, mask with a shape or apply Instant Alpha here (make colors transparent). In Advanced, you can define an image for your current master or for all masters, set a chart and legend geometry for all masters, define as text placeholder or define as media placeholder.

Keynote – Arrange Menu

Bring Forward	⌥⇧⌘F
Bring to Front	⇧⌘F
Send Backward	⌥⇧⌘B
Send to Back	⇧⌘B
Align Objects	▶
Distribute Objects	▶
Flip Horizontally	
Flip Vertically	
Lock	⌘L
Unlock	⌥⌘L
Group	⌥⌘G
Ungroup	⌥⇧⌘G

Bring Forward, Bring to Front, Send Backward, Send to Back – Think of your slide as having many layers. Each object is in its own layer. You might to take the recently imported photo and "Send it Backward" in order to see the text that was behind it. **Align Objects** - You can align your object to the left, right, center, top, middle or bottom. **Distribute Objects** - You can distribute objects horizontally or vertically. You can flip an item horizontally or vertically.

Lock/Unlock. If you are sure the location of an item is its final spot – you can lock it in place. If you want to take a few items and move them all at once – you can select the items and chose Group. This makes them one unit. You can also Ungroup after if you want.

Keynote – View Menu

This menu determines what is shown on the screen. Navigator is on by default. You can show Outline view, slides only, rulers, guides, comments, show or hide the format bar, the Inspector, colors, etc.

Keynote – Play Menu

This menu deals with the playing of your slideshow. You can also record audio to it (Record Slideshow), Rehearse and have access to the Customize Presenter Display... This window is shown below.

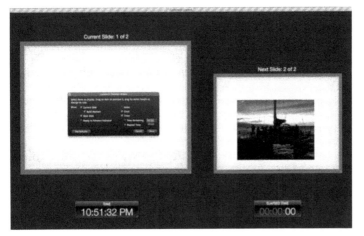

Customize Presenter Display…

Notice the play window in the first slide in the example to right. It is this window that sets what is to be seen or unseen.

Keynote – Window Menu

Minimize ⌘M
Zoom Window

Bring All to Front

✓ Untitled

This menu deals with the overall Keynote screen. **Minimize** – collapses your work and places a small icon of it on your dock. To bring it back – just click on the same icon in your dock. **Zoom Window** – expands your document until the complete document is showing on your screen. **Bring all to front** – If you have many apps open – this will take all of your open Keynote documents and bring them to the "top" of your other work. If you have more than one item open, you can toggle through them by selecting their name at the bottom of this menu. In the example, I only have one called "Untitled" open.

Keynote –Share Menu

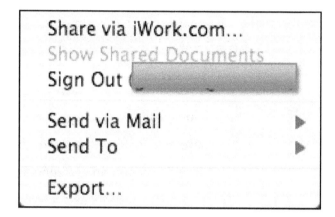

Here you can share it with iWork.com (beta). You can send it via email. You can send it to iDVD, iPhoto, iTunes, iWeb, Garageband or YouTube. You can export to a variety of formats. These include – QuickTime, PPT, PDF, Images, HTML or for an iPod.

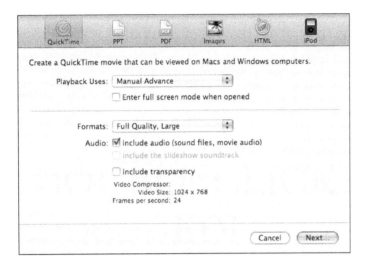

The export window is shown to the left.

Keynote – Help Menu

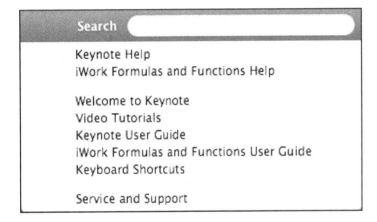

This menu is very useful. As I have said before, this guide is there to get you up and running as soon as possible and let you know what is what and where it is. For further help, please go here. You can help via typing in a word (shown below), going to Video Tutorials, accessing the User guide or iWork formulas and Functions User Guide.

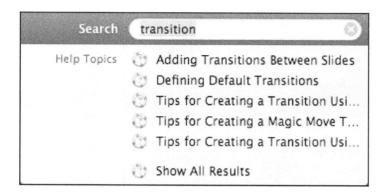

To sum up....some things look familiar....some things are new. As with the other iWork applications, I feel learning these new items will make your future work easier and of course – much more COOL!!!

Final Thoughts

I hope you found my brief guide to all of the iWork applications helpful and informative. This suite of software brings a whole new way of doing routine documents that will make you the most productive and creative person you can be. Have fun while doing work – now that's a good goal to achieve!!

www.ingramcontent.com/pod-product-compliance
Lightning Source LLC
Chambersburg PA
CBHW060456060326
40689CB00020B/4545